Finding me

HOW TO FIND YOURSELF, LOVE YOURSELF AND BE YOURSELF

By

Betty D. Higgs

Introduction

The best and most significant experience of our lives is finding who we truly are. However, so many of us stroll around either not exactly knowing or paying attention to a horrendous internal pundit that gives us every one of some unacceptable thoughts regarding ourselves. We erroneously consider self-figuring out egocentrism, and we continue without losing the main inquiry we'll at any point inquire: Who am I truly?

Winding up may seem like an intrinsically narcissistic objective, however really an unselfish cycle is at the foundation of all that we do throughout everyday life. To be the most significant individual to our general surroundings, the best accomplice, parent, and so forth, we need to initially know what our identity is, what we esteem, and, in actuality, what we bring to the table. This individual excursion is one each individual will profit from taking. A cycle includes separating - shedding layers that don't serve us in our lives and don't reflect who we truly are. However, it likewise includes a colossal demonstration of developing - perceiving who we need to be and enthusiastically approaching satisfying our one-of-a-kind predetermination - no matter what. It's a question of perceiving our own power, yet being open and defenseless against our encounters. It isn't something worth talking about to fear or stay away from, castigating ourselves en route, but instead something to search out with the interest and sympathy we would have toward a captivating new companion.

At one point throughout everyday life, you might feel like now is the right time to have a strong handle on what your identity and what makes you, indeed, you. In any case, that is a remarkable cycle (and one that is more difficult than one might expect) because carving out yourself requires opportunity and persistence.

What's the significance here to track down yourself?

While it's justifiable that you'd need to sort out what truly compels you to tick, there's compelling reason need to overreact on the off chance that you feel as if you don't have the foggiest idea, with 100% conviction, what your identity is, no matter what your age. "We all have a feeling that there is a valid, legitimate self that I need to find, and it's a mission that is essentially a long-lasting excursion toward credibility

"To wind up first find out about yourself." Finding the genuine you is an illuminating encounter. You become independent and get things done for yourself, for once. It's a hard inclination to really express, however when you don't have the foggiest idea what your identity is, it's difficult to disregard.

Winding up is difficult, however, it's worth the effort. Are you ready? Let's begin

TABLE OF CONTENT

- ❖ CHAPTER 1
- ❖ CHAPTER 2
- ❖ CHAPTER 3
- ❖ CHAPTER 4
- ❖ CHAPTER 5
- ❖ CHAPTER 6

CHAPTER 1

The lowdown of self-love

As a section step towards taking care of oneself, focus on your viewpoints and sentiments

Your psyche can be your nearest partner or your most horrendously terrible adversary. How frequently has the minuscule pundit in your mind kept you down? Your considerations can elevate your state of mind or cut it crashing down, says therapist and instructor Dr. Preetika Chandna. Taking care of oneself, she accepts, is focusing on your viewpoints and sentiments every day of your life

Taking care of yourself includes supporting your psychological well-being, practicing good eating habits, being genuinely dynamic, creating mindfulness, and keeping away from gambles with that could debilitate your prosperity.

Cherishing yourself can be extreme. It is feasible to be thoughtful to yourself when the sun's sparkling, however taking care of oneself can be an intense everyday practice to follow when nothing's turning out well for you.

Rehearsing taking care of oneself can help work on your psychological, close-to-home, physical, and otherworldly prosperity with the goal that you can depend on yourself when you really want to most. Taking care of oneself can be an incredible asset when it is placed into utilization as a day-to-day indication of exercises and ways of behaving that support your spirit, as opposed to as a crisis contingency plan. Dr. Chandna gives you a lowdown on taking care of oneself: how you can be your own fair and foul climate companion.

Practice is progress

Quieting your internal pundit requires practice. Attempt a straightforward activity. What do you see when you check out at yourself in the mirror? Is it true or not that you are speedy to recoil at your imperfections, or do you grin at your appearance? Tolerating yourself, imperfections and everything is the most important move towards really focusing on yourself. What's more, that takes practice. Take a stab at talking kind words to yourself in the mirror. Let yourself know you are cherished and acknowledged. Over the long run, contemplating your disposition, body, and sentiments become a propensity. Attempting times will appear to be more straightforward to defeat when you develop a propensity for taking a gander at yourself with acknowledgment and without judgment.

Pick you

At the point when you are confronted with a requesting chief or a domineering companion, it is not difficult to slip into human satisfying mode. Dealing with the requirements of everybody around you could leave next to no time for taking care of oneself! Focus on your requirements by permitting yourself to say a reverberating 'no!' to others when you feel overpowered. It can feel self-centered to think about yourself above others, be that as it may, running against the norm, and not taking care of your requirements is narrow-minded! That is because nobody will see the most focused on the adaptation of you!

Get some downtime
FOMO is a genuine trepidation, and every minute of everyday web-based entertainment commotion is a reality. Enjoying some time off can feel like an exercise in futility. Be that as it may, brief breaks can assist with restoring the psyche and body and assist you with performing

better working or at home. Taking care of oneself break is fundamental to re-energize and acquire a point of view when you are feeling hindered by work pressure, relationship inconveniences, childcare issues, etc. Investigate a couple of simple tips on how you can turn off and quickly return more grounded:

Switch off your mobile phone before resting and at eating times.
Take a short walk.
Take a couple of full breaths at regular intervals.
Loosen up!
Go home for the day (no disgrace in that).
Pay attention to your main tune.
Peruse a couple of pages of a book.

Connect with assistance
At the point when stress and bitterness appear a lot to deal with, it assists with contacting a confided-in companion or specialist for help. You could feel that

requesting help is an indication of shortcomings or weakness and choose to manage life's difficulties alone. Getting past difficult stretches alone is a considerable undertaking and can exhaust your close-to-home assets. Working your concerns out with an expert or companion goes quite far in making you feel significantly better, managing dissatisfactions, and reviving your assets.

Develop versatility
You can't prevent life from tossing difficulties your way, however, you can conquer them by developing your close-to-home spring-back limit or flexibility. There are a couple of compelling exercises by which you can foster versatility and energize wellbeing during stress, for example,

Move your body - work out, do yoga, go for a stroll.
Settle on quality food decisions.

Rest for seven to eight hours a day to day.
Hydrate as often as possible.
Value yourself.
Foster appreciation for others.
Put down private and expert stopping points.
Disengage from web-based entertainment now and again.
Enjoy your leisure activities.
Set a positive day-to-day certification.
Invest energy with steady individuals

Social help is the foundation of solid connections. A companion or cherished one whom you can rest on during trouble can lift you out of the most profound hopelessness.
Focusing on and participating in strong connections cause you to have an uplifting perspective on yourself. Sustain companionships that are non-judgemental and give close-to-home food.

A little guilty pleasure won't ever be stung

Carving out an opportunity to enjoy a bit of personal time is only an approach to saying you care about yourself. A spa arrangement, a day at the motion pictures, and some espresso with a companion can assist with floating your spirits when you are feeling worn out or focused. Find a movement that makes you blissful and assists you with reestablishing your physical and mental self.

At the point when life makes them hit every one of the pinion wheels, the principal thing to be thrown through the window is taking care of oneself. Top off the tank of self-esteem every now and again to try not to feel emptied out inwardly, genuinely, intellectually, and profoundly. Focus on taking care of oneself arrangement that assists you with building mental fortitude and credibility to manage life's obstacles before you arrive at a limit.

CHAPTER 2

Finding your self out of Heartbreak

The termination of your friendship, regardless of whether the end was terrible, doesn't imply that your adoration was good for nothing. Your adoration has significance regardless of whether your cherished was not deserving of your affection. To comprehend this is to start to set your most profound self towards the way of recuperating.

Search Inside
At the point when you say 'There is no adoration', then, at that point, you are without a doubt incapable to see the affection inside you.

Love conceives love and skepticism breeds disconnection. To break liberated from this twisting of antagonism, you need to cherish it once more. You are trusting that an explanation will cherish. For what reason would it be advisable for me I love once more, you ask (deliberately or subliminally)?

Be that as it may, you fail entirely to understand the situation. The issue is that you have for a long time truly needed a justification behind adoration. A concentration for your adoration, an outside wellspring of adoration. Be that as it may, love is inside you and has forever been inside you.

Obviously, we live in a period where the best bits of insight have become platitudes, and when I express a search for affection inside yourself some of you might excuse the thought as a New Age buzzword that amounts to nothing. Keep a receptive outlook and pose yourself this inquiry: When you become hopelessly enamored, where are the inclination and feelings coming from? From you, without a doubt.

Indeed, you feel that your adoration is for another, and consequently, in some way or another this feeling has a place with the other. The facts confirm that the other individual evoked this inclination inside you. Be that as it may, the individual in question was only the impetus.

When the flash of adoration was lighted, by the presence of the other, you start to feel that you will feel this just when you're with the other individual. What you want is another impetus, another flash, to light the affection that is inside you, and this time you won't tragically accept that the adoration you feel is from the other individual. You will realize that affection is a gift from the universe to every single one of us, and eventually, at our actual center, every single one of us is love.

But since we don't have the foggiest idea about this, we look for wonderful love and acknowledgment all over the place, and each time we neglect to get it, we accept that we should look once more. Deplorability is a chance for you to quit searching for adoration and to start the method involved with cherishing yourself once more.

To feel and interface with your center of adoration, work through the activities for recuperating the body, then, at that point, work through excruciating feelings like apprehension, depression, and disgrace. You are then prepared to interface with adoration.

Going Deeper
Sometime in the past, you felt significantly better about yourself. You felt acknowledged for what your identity was. You didn't think about yourself with regards to great and terrible - as a matter of fact, you didn't think about yourself by any stretch of the

imagination. All Your requirements were dealt with, and you felt warm and get.

We have all accomplished unadulterated happiness in our mom's belly. You don't deliberately recollect the experience, however, someplace inside you is the close-to-home memory of being washed in warm liquid, all your requirements are taken care, of being acknowledged, and feeling content with yourself. Before you were conceived (and for some time later), you had no clue about yourself as a person. You and the universe were one, joined in happiness.

Vedanta lets us know that you are the universe - unadulterated, immortal, everlasting, and complete - and that you can associate with your real essence through reflection and consideration. Then again, you are adding a person. An individual with a name, an appearance, a character, and a task to carry out in the public eye.

Out past thoughts of bad behavior and right-doing,

there is a field. I'll meet you there.

At the point when the spirit rests in that grass,

the world is too full to even consider discussing.

Thoughts, language, and even the expression 'each other' has neither rhyme nor reason.

At the point when 'you' are harmed, Vedanta tells us, it is just the possibility of you, the singular self, that is wounded by deplorability.
Your singular self accepts that you want the other for satisfaction. It is frightened of being separated from everyone else. Your psyche is misdirected by want and dread,

and fools you into feeling that you are fragmented without her/him.
Be that as it may, our antiquated texts remind us, that you can interface with your genuine self - not who you assume you are, not the name you connect to yourself, not your work, or your looks, or your body.

Your actual self is past craving, dread, and connection.

Your actual self then, at that point, can't be harmed.

Your actual self is the everlasting, immortal, astronomical self, one that exists a past judgment, past good and bad, great and terrible. It is consistently delighted.

Your actual self is love, harmony, and satisfaction.

Western clinicians suddenly moved toward this. They concentrated on the individual and investigated inquiries concerning what makes us extraordinary.

The East investigated the astronomical immortal self, and the West investigated the human individual self.

To genuinely change from the experience of deplorability, interface with both - the person that you are and the everlasting happiness that you are, forever was and consistently will be.

CHAPTER 3

Find self compassion

Have you at any point blown your top at... yourself? Accused and afterward beat yourself up somewhat inside for accomplishing something you lament?

Perhaps you've been unforgiving with somebody, just to be a lot more extreme with yourself later?

It's not difficult to be hard on yourself — we will quite often do it a whole lot more than we understand. Be that as it may, imagine a scenario in which there was a superior way. At the point when we pardon ourselves, acknowledge our apparent imperfections, and offer ourselves grace, we practice self-sympathy. It's generally expected significantly more enthusiastically than it sounds, however with the right strategies, we can figure out how to make it a propensity that sticks.

Self-sympathy is an inspirational perspective we can have towards ourselves, and it's likewise an observationally quantifiable development.
Having self-sympathy implies having the option to connect with yourself in a manner that is pardoning, tolerating, and cherishing when circumstances maybe not exactly ideal. We know that it's like (yet less long-lasting than) self-esteem and that it's unmistakable from confidence, yet how would we show self-sympathy?

Self-Kindness
Self-thoughtfulness is tied in with offering grace and understanding toward ourselves when we come up short at something, or when we are harmed as opposed to being basic or making a decision about ourselves brutally when we now feel torment, we can perceive the adverse impact of

self-judgment and indulge ourselves with warmth and persistence all things being equal.

To put it plainly, offering self-grace implies regarding our value as unrestricted in any event, when we miss the mark concerning our assumptions, whether it's through our ways of behaving or even our considerations, giving yourself the delicacy and care you want while you're going through a difficult stretch;
Attempting to comprehend and show persistence concerning your apparent character imperfections; and
Being open-minded toward your inadequacies.

Normal Humanity

'Being essential for something greater' is an unavoidable idea in certain brain research writing, and it's for quite some time been contended that the requirement for associations is important for human instinct. Having Common Humanity implies seeing our singular encounters as implanted in the more extensive human experience, as opposed to considering ourselves to be disconnected or separate from others.

Some portion of this is tolerating and pardoning ourselves for our imperfections — we are more than a little flawed, however, we show self-sympathy when we ease off of ourselves for having restrictions. One more piece of normal humankind is understanding that we're in good company to be blemished or feeling hurt; as opposed to pulling out or disconnecting ourselves, we value that others feel something very similar now and again.

Seeing your deficiencies as regular parts of the human condition;
Seeing your challenges as "a piece of life that everybody goes through"; and

Advising yourself that others additionally feel insufficient now and again, when you feel something very similar.

Care
Care is viewed as something contrary to aversion or over-distinguishing proof in the self-sympathy hypothesis — it involves recognizing and marking our contemplations rather than responding to them.

At the point when we have self-sympathy, we know about our destructive contemplations and feelings without exploding their importance through rumination. All things being equal, we embrace a good harmony between this over-distinguishing proof at one limit, and keeping away from excruciating feelings and encounters at the other, expecting to keep our sentiments in balance when we experience something disturbing;

Keeping up with the point of view when we come up short at things that are essential to us; and
Embracing our feelings with interest and receptiveness when we feel miserable.
So while the SCS estimates self-sympathy as a characteristic, it can likewise be viewed as a 'balance' or a 'center method' of close-to-home answering.

Tips and Techniques for Practicing Self-Compassion

There are bunches of explicit activities accessible that will assist you with rehearsing self-sympathy that suits you.

Indulge Yourself as You'd Treat a Friend

One great spot to begin is by contemplating how you would treat others that you care about. So while we can't generally remove others' aggravation, we can approve its presence and offer help to assist them with getting past it and developing. In this regard:

Allow yourself to commit errors.

Self-thoughtfulness and normal mankind tap into two separate however related thoughts: "We're human. In any case, a) so is every other person, and b) that is OK." Rather than understanding our considerations, sentiments, and ways of behaving as what our identity is, we can let ourselves free when we could do likewise for other people. On the off chance that a companion gets lethargic and doesn't answer your call, you most likely will not in a split second accept for the time being that they're a terrible individual. Allowing yourself to be human every so often is one method for tolerating your blemishes, and advising yourself that you're in good company to be defective.

Care for yourself as you'd treat others.

Firmly connected with the past tip, this is tied in with being understanding and compassionate towards yourself. On the off chance that a companion is feeling down, hurt, or upset, you could genuinely congratulate them or hold their hand. Neff portrays these as approaches to taking advantage of our own 'providing care framework' to deliver oxytocin which has valuable cardiovascular impacts alongside delicate, pardoning language (in any event, utilizing affectionate nicknames to yourself like "dear" or "darling"), these motions can lead us to feeling self-thoughtfulness regardless of whether we're at first hesitant. Do whatever it takes not to get carried away with the charming terms if it feels excessively odd!
Turning out to be More Self-Aware

Different procedures connect with being more mindful and taking advantage of our self-talk. Contrasted with 'thrashing ourselves for pummeling ourselves', becoming mindful of our interior stories is a positive beginning stage for changing our self-talk.

Use 'Putting out Announcements'. Perhaps you've never loved positive certifications. Perhaps they don't feel regular or you accept they don't exactly 'come to your Inner Critic at a psyche level, If that is the situation, you could attempt what is conversationally alluded to as 'putting out announcements. These are firmly related (on the off chance that not the same) to smaller than expected practices in self-absolution and tap into the care idea of disconnected non-judgment. At the point when you discover yourself thinking a pessimistic idea like "I'm a particularly horrendous individual for flying off the handle", take a stab at turning it around and 'setting' yourself free from the inclination. All things being equal, attempt "It's alright that I felt upset".

Attempt self-acknowledgment. This implies embracing your apparent deficiencies as well as your personality assets.

Self-sympathy is about not over-blowing up these inadequacies into a meaning of what our identity is — rather, considerations and sentiments are ways of behaving and states.

Practice care. Harvard Healthbeat (2019) recommends that care rehearses are an effective method for focusing on time. In addition to the fact that mindfulness is one of the self-sympathy center's development, however a ton of activities, for example, yoga and profound breathing can be utilized whenever, anyplace. Kirstin Neff likewise suggests directed supporting contemplations, including body examines and a short 'Self-Compassion Break'.

Do whatever it takes not to pass judgment on yourself excessively fast. Another tip is to quit expecting you'll act a specific way. It's not difficult to expect things like "I get truly cantankerous and standoffish on flights", which some of the time blocks the likelihood that you'll act an alternate way. This is by and by about regarding yourself as you would others, and simply a future-zeroed method for assuming the best about yourself.

(Re)Gaining Perspective

Yet again from here, we can likewise zoom out to advise ourselves that we're associated with others. That we're essential for a lot greater picture — normal humankind — and change our concentrate in like manner. Here are some model tips:

Relinquish the requirement for outside approval. Creator Dani DiPirro of Stay Positive, The Positively Present Guide to Life recommends that bunches of our negative reasoning come from how others see us. On the off chance that we're thrashing ourselves for eating something, for example, a great deal of that independent displeasure comes from prevailing difficulties, similar to the strain to look a specific way or keep a specific weight. Deciding not to attach our satisfaction to outside impacts can in this manner be a demonstration of self-thoughtfulness with a lot bigger thump on impact.

Connecting with others. This could seem like something contrary to the abovementioned, however, as a matter of fact, this procedure is more about setting your sentiments in the setting. At the point when we talk with others, we understand that we're in good company to feel torment at various times. It's a significant piece of reaffirming our feeling of connectedness, reevaluating our apparent issues inside the 'master plan, and building socially encouraging groups of people that are important to prosperity.

CHAPTER 4

Release self doubt

It's generally expected to encounter sensations of uncertainty when we are confronted with new or testing circumstances. Self-question is described by sensations of vulnerability regarding at least one part of oneself. It is something that we as a whole might insight at specific times in our lives. In any case, when it becomes crippling for us, that is the point at which we might require more apparatuses to beat self-question.

Self-uncertainty might come from past bad encounters or connection style issues. Those with shaky connections might have experienced being censured, which can add to self-question sometime down the road.

Assuming somebody has been told in the past that they're "not sufficient" or unequipped for something, then, at that point, this can affect their self-esteem. We likewise have a profound cultural strain to accomplish, which can be more hurtful than persuading for us.

On the off chance that relentless self-question isn't tended to, it can prompt:

- Tension
- Gloom
- Lingering or absence of inspiration
- Profound shakiness
- Low confidence
- Trouble deciding

What is Imposter Syndrome?

An inability to embrace success remains inseparable from self-question. Clinicians portray it as the experience of feeling like a cheat, despite having made progress. An inability to acknowledge success is something particularly felt among ladies and minority gatherings. An inability to acknowledge success can restrict our fortitude to place ourselves out there in a significant manner or pursue new open doors. It brings up individuals to encounter self-question on the off chance that they are "Sufficiently qualified" or doing "alright," in a task, a relationship, a companionship, as a parent, or some other movement (even though they generally are).

Self-uncertainty and an inability to embrace success can meaningfully affect somebody's confidence. Notwithstanding, there are ways of combatting these sentiments and becoming more sure about ourselves and our capacities.

Instructions to Overcome Self-Doubt

1. Practice Self-Compassion

On the off chance that self-question is keeping you away from taking a jump with your vocation or in one more part of your life, it assists with recollecting that we are human. We as a whole commit errors en route and it's OK to do as such. At the point when we question our capacities, it's frequently because we would rather not set aside any space for botches. In any case, botches are likewise how we learn and develop. We can moderate self-uncertainty and apprehension about disappointment by working on being thoughtful to ourselves, regardless of the result.

2. Remember Your Past Achievements

Recollect when you might have been terrified to follow through with something, in your everyday schedule, except it truly wound up going all around well. It assists with pondering substantial accomplishments where something trying for us transformed into something extraordinary. A ton of accomplishments are conceived out of starting vulnerability or uncertainty. It assists with reminding ourselves about the times that things have gone right because the same thing could occur right now.

On the other side, it's great to not zero in a lot on the past or past disappointments we could have had. The current second is another amazing chance to do admirably, regardless of whether things go right the initial time.

3. Try to Not Compare Yourself to Others

They say that correlation is the hoodlum of delight. This idiom sounds accurate in numerous ways. If you're encountering self-question since you're apprehensive you will not achieve something at a similar level as another person, then, at that point, it tends to be a deadening inclination. Everybody's excursions and thoughts of achievement are unique. What we have some control over and center around is our way and where we need to take it, paying little mind to where others are at or what they have done.

4. Be Mindful of Your Thinking

At the point when negative considerations start to sneak in, now and again they are difficult to perceive because we become so used to them. An inability to acknowledge success flourishes off of these negative contemplations that let us know that we aren't deserving of the spot we're at or that we won't deliver great work. Next time these contemplations continue, inquire as to whether you truly accept that they are valid. Consider how positive reasoning might move your outlook and permit you to be more certain about your capacities.

5. Spend Time With Supportive People

The loved ones in our lives who have faith in us and all that we're equipped for will continuously be our allies. While you're feeling self-question, encircle yourself with these individuals. They can help you to remember how capable and strong you are during times when you're not having that impression about yourself.

6. Find Validation From Within

While it's perfect to feel consoled by others that we are working hard or that we are fit for achieving a troublesome errand, having our confidence in ourselves is similarly significant. Steady consolation means practically nothing if we don't have confidence in ourselves. Regardless of whether we aren't the most certain about where we're at, it's great to work on tolerating our assets and all that we bring to the table.

7. Remember That You're The Harshest Critic

Could you question a companion who accepted another position or how they parent their children the same way that you question yourself.? The response is reasonable no. We will continuously be the most brutal pundit for ourselves. It's a decent suggestion to treat ourselves with the very thoughtfulness and sympathy that we have for other people, rather than being so basic on ourselves.

8. Identify Your Values

Pause for a minute to evaluate your qualities and what makes the biggest difference to you. You may be thoughtful to other people, you're an old buddy, or you add to something significant in your life. At the point when we perceive these qualities as the main thing to us, the apprehension about analysis from others drops off the radar. Furthermore, when we live lined up with our qualities, it doesn't feel as hindering to be condemned or commit errors.

9. Keep a Journal

Journaling is generally a helpful activity to rehearse. Recording your contemplations of self-uncertainty or encounters with an inability to embrace success onto paper may be a decent delivery. You might try and acknowledge after you see your interests down on paper, that they may not be all around as adverse as you suspected they were. This can serve to conquer self-question continuously.

10. Seek Professional Help

It might assist with seeing psychological well-being proficient to defeat self-question if these sentiments persevere to the point that makes it hard for you to work in daily existence. Treatment can assist us with feeling comprehended and give us devises to ease sensations of uncertainty. Mental conduct treatment (CBT) is a famous type of treatment that can help explicitly with self-question. With CBT, we can learn techniques to challenge dangerous perspectives that might prompt a superior state of mind and by and large prosperity.

CHAPTER 5

Embrace who you are

Embrace what your identity is and your heavenly reason. Distinguish the obstructions in your day-to-day existence, and foster discipline, mental fortitude, and the solidarity to for all time move past them, and continue to push ahead." "Embrace those pieces of yourself that you've ably kept away from up to this point. That is your experience.

In some cases, in any case, there's nobody around to give you that embrace you want. While you're having a terrible day, encountering an aggravation of some kind, or essentially wanting a touch of fondness, why not give affection to yourself? ... Mimic the strain that you feel when you get a consoling huge squeeze.

There is such a great amount to you than meets the eye. Valid, you might not have sorted out about yourself but rather you can in any case expand on the little you know. Try not to allow individuals to close you down since they could do without how you talk or your sort of thoughts. Try not to allow individuals to put you down since you are not what they anticipate. Try not to recoil since you need to cause somebody to feel great around you. Try not to become another person since somebody close could do without your sort of individual. It is the kind of person you are, embrace it and make its best.

You need to quit saying 'sorry' for what your identity is. You can't continue to deny what your interests are, regardless of who misconception matters to you. You ought to be your main fan, nobody ought to cherish you more than you love yourself. Your line of consideration might appear to be exceptionally odd, don't be timid to remain your thought process is genuine, and be pleased with your perspectives. You might not have as many bits of knowledge as others do however that doesn't mean you are not equipped for something more significant. There is a You in there, embrace it.

You can get the hang of it, learning isn't past you. You can enhance your ongoing self that is living however never let anybody remove your qualities and what you accept. These are your character, battle to keep them, they are what your identity is, safeguard them with your life. You are unique never allowed anybody to let you know if not, in any event, when individuals neglect to see the reason why never question yourself. They will doubtlessly come around, everyone with goodies in hand gifts when you completely structure.

Love yourself, nobody will do that ideal for you. Try not to let your head down fewer others will peer down on you. Lowliness is great yet does it with satisfaction, self-conviction, confidence, great confidence, and unshaken longing to succeed regardless. You are your own most noteworthy partner, cast away all questions and pay attention to your gut feelings, stand by listening to your heart and give close consideration to your mindset. They are all important for your making, in any event, when your eyes neglect to see they will keep you protected and on target.

Make everything about you, when you figure out how to cherish yourself as you ought to, adoring others won't be an issue. This will influence your kinship and relationship; it takes a total of you to supplement another. You have such a great amount inside you; ability, gift, insight, contemplations, energy... cherishing yourself is all you want to enhance every one of these. Try not to bomb the You inside, embrace what your identity is, and watch life get less muddled.

Assemble yourself

Developing yourself is important before you fabricate anything. At times you are broken and you want to remake yourself up from nothing. Now and again you need to begin new to assemble yourself from nothing.

You want to appropriately figure out how to construct yourself. You might be toward the start or you are broken and you want to reconstruct yourself. Developing yourself is extremely fundamental for carrying on with a cheerful life.

Try not to surrender trust. You can turn out to be better by dealing with yourself for some time. You want extraordinary assurance and self-assurance to construct yourself. Be confident and follow the interaction.

There are two sections in this course of developing you:

Mentality:
(I) You should try to understand that you can't change your past. Acknowledge this and continue. Try not to choose not to move on that is proceeded to quit agonizing over the future which is on the way.

(ii) You have this life you have a decision to live and develop intellectually. Some individuals are wanting for something like one day to carry on with their lives. You are fortunate you have a life.

(iii) Find motivation from individuals who assembled themselves. Assuming that you want evidence, you can investigate individuals who assembled themselves from nothing. You can track down them from the web, books, or different assets.
When you assemble your psyche. You can utilize this basic, and strong technique to

assemble yourself, and this takes time and exertion. Along these lines, be patient and work on yourself.

Technique:
Learn and Observe: Find what you need to develop in yourself. It might be your actual body or a solid brain or it could be an expert. Anything it could be, you have a few assets accessible and effectively readily available in this cutting-edge world. You can work out each day to assemble your body. You can contemplate fabricating your care. You can find numerous assets on the ability you need to foster effectively through books, courses, or training from specialists. Make an everyday arrangement and this assists you with remaining restrained. Be predictable and avoid no day. It could be troublesome toward the start, and you might need to endure torment. It's OK. Try not to surrender and continue to chip away at yourself. See what's going on around you. Listen more than you talk. Notice

individuals' activities more. Noticing assists you with advancing normally.

Practice and Apply: Whatever you are learning and seeing in your life, practice and apply in your reality. It doesn't make any difference assuming you read 1000 books or taken 100 courses if you don't try what you realized, it's futile. Practice consistently. Apply when you are prepared. Acquire aptitude and don't be a novice. You might commit botches all the while, and it's okay. Gain from your mix-ups and don't rehash them. Work on each day by rehearsing more and telling no good reasons and recalling these reasons obliterate you. Assuming you are going through dull times, make sure to remain steadfast and accept that dim times in life are transitory. Try not to quit any pretense of building yourself anything circumstances might come.

Result: (Success or Failure) If you succeed, well done, and keep it up. Even though you did everything accurately, the outcomes may not be true to form, and in such circumstances, don't lose trust. Try not to stop developing yourself. Recollect that achievement may not occur in one go. Here and there it takes a few preliminaries. You want to grasp disappointments as a feature of your prosperity. They are showing you important examples for a fruitful life and they assist you with building areas of strength that are fundamental for building yourself so solid. Continue to work until you succeed and couldn't care less about others' judgment and assessment. Try not to surrender in light of circumstances. Demonstrate to the existence that you are more grounded than your circumstances. Be patient and you will get what you need.

Rehash: Once you have fabricated one thing you need. You might have different things to work on in your life and apply the cycle. Remain inspired, and this assists you with building yourself more quickly.

CHAPTER 6

Do what you love and love what you do

You've heard the well-known axiom, "Make every moment count and you won't ever work a day in that frame of mind." In numerous ways, this colloquialism is valid. On the off chance that you're enthusiastic about what you do and you're investing your concentration and time into it, you won't feel like you're working. However many individuals blame this belief system. Why invested energy and exertion into something on the off chance that you don't cherish it?

Truly, on the off chance that you love how you make ends meet, you have most likely begun by finding a way few ways to arrive at that objective. A great many people don't enter their professions and promptly have an enthusiasm for the business. What is the

IT factor these individuals share for all intents and purposes? Reason. On the off chance that you utilize your feeling of direction to illuminate your expert choices and progress, you will wind up showing yourself how to live life to the fullest.

To truly be consistent with your motivation as it connects with your all-consuming purpose, which is critical to building a profession in which you genuinely love what you do, then, at that point, you want to ask yourself, "What is my internal potential, and what are my most profound abilities?" By investigating questions that push you to find your personality, values, and what you care about the most, you'll track down your reality: you should initially comprehend what your actual gift is to track down satisfaction in your vocation.

As Tony Robbins says, "Change is programmed, however, progress isn't. If you have any desire to gain ground, you want an arrangement, a methodology, and progressing propensities to obtain the outcomes you need." We'll separate these parts and examine how they're fundamental if you have any desire to do what you endlessly love you do.

FIGURE OUT HOW TO DO WHAT YOU LOVE

If you're overpowered by the possibility of rolling out extraordinary improvements to live the dream and get paid for the privilege, make child strides. Getting to realize yourself is the most important phase in figuring out how to cherish what you do. Here are far to reach out to what motivates you.

1. CENTRE AROUND YOUR STRENGTHS

Before you can figure out how to live life to the fullest, you should understand what it is that you love to do! This is a course of self-disclosure that places you in contact with your fundamental beliefs, assets, and resources. In his Building the Ultimate Business Advantage course, advertising master Jay Abraham expresses that numerous business visionaries are despondent because they are continually attempting to work on their shortcomings. Jay advocates zeroing in on your assets while concluding what kind of business to begin and setting up a development methodology. At the point when you distinguish what you appreciate doing and the exercises you're ready to dominate moderately rapidly, you'll accomplish more significant victories that lead to satisfaction.

Making a profession where you live the dream and get paid for the privilege is tied in with investing most of your energy rehearsing and following up on your assets. This isn't simply a recipe for expanding your enthusiasm for business, either - when potential clients perceive how enthusiastic you are, they're bound to get on, which emphatically builds your likelihood of business achievement.

2. TRACK DOWN YOUR PASSIONS

The subsequent stage in fostering a profession wherein you love what you do is in thinking obviously about your motivation. What engages you? What do you want to awaken and do consistently? These responses should conform to what your assets are. For certain individuals, the capacity to do the very thing you love implies helping other people. For an alternate individual, it's offering their viewpoints and sentiments imaginatively. Others esteem travel or investing energy with their loved ones. When you've truly contemplated what carrying on with an unprecedented life resembles for you, consider how you'll accomplish it.

3. CONVERSE WITHA CAREER COUNSELOR

Working with a professional instructor is a magnificent method for fining tune your vocation way. Professional advocates are prepared to direct clients in the most ideal bearing toward self-realization. A talented professional instructor assesses your abilities, foundation, motivations, and character qualities to assist with modifying a game plan to live life to the fullest.

4 FABRICATE YOUR NETWORK

At the point when you're currently changing your profession to live life to the fullest, this is an ideal opportunity to make associations and extend your organization. At the point when you connect with others - particularly individuals you regard who've found replies to how to live life to the fullest - you tap into an asset of help, data, and motivation. Then, at that point, when you go to carry out your methodology for professional satisfaction, your organization will be all set.

5. SET ASIDE CASH

As you work to fabricate a profession that allows you to live life to the fullest, be vital about your funds so your assets are centered around the award. Focus on your spending on exercises that help your interests. You'll expand your healthy identity viability while holding assets to accomplish your fantasies.

CARRING OUT A STRATEGY TO LOVE WHAT YOU DO

You've proactively invested the leg effort important to live life to the fullest. Your subsequent stage is coming up with a methodology for arriving. This is your activity plan for figuring out how to do what you endlessly love what you do.

1. TO LOVE WHAT YOU DO, STRATEGIZE WISELY

Except if you're naturally introduced to cash, you must attempt to have the option to live life to the fullest. Begin with an arrangement - or even better, a Massive Action Plan. How might you accomplish your actual reason through work? How might you consolidate that interest with a certifiable profession? Plan how you can make your vision a reality.

You're never going to go from point A, as an all-out fledgling, to point Z, in which you supernaturally get to live life to the fullest and have accomplished total independence from the rat race. You need to plan shrewdly to go from point A to direct B toward point C, etc. How might you most proficiently fabricate a profession wherein you love what you do? There are a couple of steps you can take to facilitate this interaction:

TRACK DOWN A MENTOR:

Whether it's somebody you know, in actuality, who has made monstrous progress or somebody you haven't met face to face yet extraordinarily appreciate, figure out how they made progress. Ask them what steps they took to find how to live life to the fullest, then, at that point, ask yourself how you can demonstrate the way they took with acclimations to meet your particular conditions. Pretty much every effective financial specialist - including Tony - has been instructed by coaches all through their professions.

WORK WITH A COACH:

On the off chance that you don't have the mastery to live life to the fullest and fabricate a business around it all alone, simply sit back and relax: There is a lot of help accessible. Work with a Results Coach who can assist you with zeroing in on your ultimate objective and help you in fostering a well-thought-out course of action to arrive at it.

Enhance:

While you're making progress toward your objective of having a profession where you live life to the fullest, you will experience difficulties and disappointment - that is unavoidable. The key is to transform those difficulties into victories by zeroing in on consistent and vital advancement. How might you refine your methodology? How might you change how you're treating others all the more quickly to meet your objective?

On the off chance that you don't know what methodology to utilize, think about utilizing every one of the three: focusing on development in your expert existence with the assistance of a mentor or tutor. Research shows that this blend of responsibility and mentorship is one of the best ways of building a profession in which you live life to the fullest. Thirty years of examination on the subject evaluated 43 investigations contrasting profession results of individuals who either connected with coaches or didn't in that frame of mind of vocation advancement. The individuals who drew in coaches got higher remuneration, and more advancements felt happier with (and focused on) their professions and felt bound to appreciate future professional success. One more overview of 170 experts found that the individuals who connected with coaches were fundamentally bound to see the value in their work environment and its administration. Connecting with a coach likewise influenced representative standards for dependability and representatives' feelings of consideration in the working environment, the two of which become possibly the most important factor concerning professional satisfaction.

2. FOSTER POSITIVE HABITS

It might take some time for you to live life to the fullest at work and make money at it, so you want to ensure you're creating maintainable propensities during the interaction. This incorporates proficient propensities, such as turning into an extraordinary organizer and consistently going to courses to better your abilities, and individual ones, such as guaranteeing you're getting some much-needed rest to live life to the fullest beyond work, such as paying attention to engaging digital recordings and investing energy with your children. At the point when rehearsed consistently over the long haul, these propensities will support you in any event, when circumstances become difficult. As your expert process advances, you can continuously return to these acquired and developed abilities.

Creating good propensities will likewise assist you with making an agreeable balance between fun and serious activities, which will thusly upgrade your sensations of satisfaction once you are in a profession in which you love what you do. How does orchestrating your own proficient lives improve your profession? Research exhibits that it is the balance between fun and serious activities, not cash, independence, or even acknowledgment, which at last drives professional achievement. In particular, an overview of 4,100 business leaders from medium-to-enormous firms in 33 nations uncovered that, when representatives can adjust their expert and individual lives, they connect undeniably more promptly with the jobs needing to be done (and the group with which they team up) than workers who are exhausted. This feeling of balance between serious and fun activities results not just in that frame of mind from a given organization yet additionally in representatives feeling like they "have everything" with regards to all-encompassing life satisfaction. Take their signal and attempt to orchestrate your work existence with your own life.

3. INCREMENT YOUR PASSION FOR BUSINESS BY FALLING IN LOVE WITH YOUR CLIENTS

Regardless of how much enthusiasm for a business you create, there will in any case be undertakings you don't completely appreciate and days when you question your plan of action. What pushes you along during circumstances such as these and assists you with proceeding to cherish what you do? Jay recommends that building a profession where you do the very thing you love involves experiencing passionate feelings for your clients. At the point when you take the concentration off your items and administrations and put it on what your business means for the existence of those you serve, you can cherish what you in all actuality do in any event, during the most unremarkable undertakings. Jay states you want to lose the drive to make your organization the "greatest" or "generally well known" and on second thought be enthusiastic about the effect you have on your clients' lives. Make each reach you have with clients an opportunity to dive more deeply into their qualities, expectations, and dreams and become their confided-in consultant for how to get what they need. At the point when you understand your client's life is your business life, you comprehend that becoming hopelessly enamored with them touches off your enthusiasm for the business.

Having the option to live the dream and get paid for the privilege is conceivable, however, it requires investment. Choose today to begin pursuing your objectives, and understand that there are many strides en route between where you start and where you need to be. In particular, develop propensities that fill your existence with satisfaction as you venture down the way to progress.

4. GIVE YOURSELF CREDIT FOR WANTING TO DO WHAT YOU LOVE

Making change takes mental fortitude, and that is the precise exact thing you're doing when you take steps to live life to the fullest. Rather than taking the path of least resistance and making do with the state of affairs, you've pursued the more respectable option to construct a day-to-day existence that motivates you.

5. VALUE YOUR MISTAKES

Figuring out how to do the very thing you love is an interaction. Oppose the compulsion to view your ongoing profession as a disappointment or misstep. All things being equal, view it as a wellspring of data - on how you would rather not be making ends meet, the qualities you created throughout your job(s), and the organization you've constructed. At the point when you're ready to gain from your missteps without pummeling yourself over them (or calling it quits), each step you move toward a day-to-day existence where you love what you do.

You have the right to have a satisfying profession that permits you to live the dream and get paid for the privilege. Uncover your internal potential and most profound abilities with our Business Identity test. Find and use your gift to track down your definitive reason for living.

CONCLUSION

Certainty and dependence are at the core of tracking down yourself. On the off chance that you don't have a strong identity worth, you'll pay attention to what others need to say constantly and be influenced by their emphasis on what is suitable. Figure out how to have confidence in yourself and trust your sentiments. Then, at that point, you'll think of construction on which to base your new identity. Keep in mind, show restraint toward yourself, and be positive about your capacities. All that will accompany time.

On the off chance that you have been defrauded previously, go up against these issues. They won't disappear all alone. They may be shading your way to deal with day-to-day existence, making you satisfy others' assumptions rather than your own.

Begin confiding in your judgment and dynamic cycles, missteps, and not. We as a whole commit error, however, through botches we think of ourselves as developing, learning, and arriving at our genuine selves.

Begin assuming a sense of ownership with planning, family matters, and arranging what's in store. Individuals who come up short on healthy identity will more often than not dismiss the "subtleties" of existence with a lighthearted disposition, accepting that things will all get themselves straightened out. Be that as it may, things don't necessarily in every case get themselves straightened out. Assuming liability pulls you back from the incline and allows you to be independent not entirely set in stone, at this point not conveyed along by the rushes of destiny.

Printed in the USA
CPSIA information can be obtained
at www.ICGtesting.com
CBHW051026221024
16228CB00026B/311